Business is War and Strategies o: Hun and A

By Emily Goldstein

©Copyright 2016 WE CANT BE BEAT LLC

Copyright 2016 by Emily Goldstein

Published by WE CANT BE BEAT LLC

Krob817@yahoo.com

Table of Contents

Introduction: 5

Chapter 1: Genghis Khan: What a Modern-Day Business Warrior Can Learn From the Greatest Conqueror of All Time: Part 1 13

Chapter 2: Genghis Khan: What a Modern-Day Business Warrior Can Learn From the Greatest Conqueror of All Time: Part 2 24

Chapter 3: The Power of Perception: Building Your Own Intimidating Personal Brand, Part 1 39

Chapter 4: The Appearance of Power: Building Your Own Intimidating Personal Brand, Part 2 46

Chapter 5: Learning From Attila the Hun: Three Critical Lessons to Elevate Your Business Battle Skills Instantly ..55

Chapter 6: The Gladiator: How to Dominate Any Arena You Enter 65

Chapter 8: Nice Guys Don't Survive The Wilderness: Lessons From the Animal World 86

Chapter 9: How to Negotiate Like a Boss: Lessons Busines Warriors can Use to Win Every Battle....................105

Chapter 10: Learning The Way of The Warrior From Alexander the Great and Genghis Khan: Make Discipline Your Discipline..117

Conclusion:..133

Introduction:

"<u>Business is war. I go out there, I want to kill the competitors. I want to make their lives miserable. I want to steal their market share. I want them to fear me and I want everyone on my team thinking we're going to win.</u>"

Kevin O'Leary, self-made multi-millionaire

This book is not an investment book. It's not a guide to gold mining in some far flung land or making big bucks from bit coins. It's about far more than that.

It's a roadmap to gaining the psychological skills and secret strategies that will help you to earn more, have more, and be more in an ultra-competitive business environment. These strategies show you that the greatest war is the one that you fight against yourself- the battle against self-doubt, fear, weakness and lack of discipline. Once you've battled these things and won- **nothing, literally nothing**, can stand in the way of you achieving your financial goals.

There are more than enough books out there promising to teach you how to invest in stocks, which business is hot this year and what startup trends you need to be aware of. These books may have great advice in them but each one is temporary, based very much on the here and now and the information they contain may not be as useful or relevant to you next year, let alone in the next decade. This book was designed to be different-drawing on the some of the greatest figures in history to provide you with a solid inner battle plan for future business success.

I always look to history for vital insight into solving today and tomorrow's problems. Why? History's lessons are enduring. They withstand the test of time and are just as potent, just as effective and just as usable today as they were thousands of years ago. You can use the tactics in this guide in the next 10 minutes, next week, next year or in 20 years from now and they will still hold true. That's what sets them apart from the usual business advice available today.

So why is it important for today's business warriors to look to the ancient world for lessons? Simply put, because the ancient world was all about the truth. In the ancient world, people had no time for the middle ground. Things were seen as right or wrong, black or white, and people were either weak or strong. In most ancient civilizations, you were a leader or a follower, a master or a peasant and there was no confusing the two roles.

There was also no attempt to disguise these facts. Today, we think civilization means lying to ourselves about the reality of our harsh existence. We create "gray areas" and come up with pretty fairytales like "everyone can be happy and everyone can win". Heck, we even give prizes to people who come in second place! In the ancient world, there was none of that nonsense. Second place was commonly understood to mean "just another person who didn't win" AKA a loser.

Now, you may be thinking-"whew! I'm glad I don't live in such a stark polemic society" but if you're really honest with yourself, you'll realize that you actually do. We are still the same human beings. Life is still a dog-eat-dog battle to the death and the ONLY thing that has changed is our willingness to be honest about it.

One major factor that sets leaders apart from the followers they control is their ability to understand these facts. Leaders know that in life, you can either be a winner or a loser, a champion or a failure and this simple understanding is a key that opens up the doors to wealth and power.

Why? Well, let's just imagine that you are involved in what you think is just a "friendly" basketball game. You believe that the game is purely for fun and that there really are no winners or losers among friends, so you probably don't try as much or play as aggressively. In the end, you wind up losing because you had the mindset that the "competition wasn't serious". Now, imagine that the entire time, that "friendly game" was actually a competition for mega-bucks and only one player really knew this. That one player would try harder, play more aggressively and behave far more strategically than all the players who believed the game didn't matter. Because that player KNEW the game counted and counted a LOT, he would be much more likely to win, at any cost.

Life is exactly the same. The majority of people view it as a "process", a long, meandering journey in which everyone, no matter how much or how little they try, ends up at roughly the same place.

Winners however, know that this isn't true. Almost from the minute that they are old enough to observe and understand the world around them, they see it for what it really is- an enormous competition in which the winner takes all! That's why these people are ultra-motivated, work harder, smarter and faster than their peers, take advantage of every opportunity that comes their way and even make opportunities for themselves in the face of adversity. They know that there IS a prize and so, while others take life calmly, work just as much (and only as much) as others, think short-term and fail to view their peers as competitors, the winners put in extra effort, they work longer and harder than you do, they think, plan and behave more strategically than you and they don't view anyone as just a peer.

Instead, they know that EVERYONE is a competitor for the same prize of money, power and security, whether they realize it or not. Winners don't ever underestimate anyone-whether it be themselves or others. Instead, they look at life the way the warriors of the ancient world did- dead on, frankly and without any illusions. This effectively helps winners to "see" the bigger picture while the rest of the world is just looking at the details. So before I get into the other business and life lessons you can learn from the leaders of the ancient world, I just want to pause and stress these three concepts: Life is a competition. Business, especially, is a zero-sum competition and the winner takes ALL. Your peers are actually your competitors. If you realize these three facts now, you will effectively be competing against people who don't even know that they are in a competition. Just imagine what kind of a winning edge this will give you! Get into this mindset today and you'll instantly have a huge advantage over those who think differently.

Now that you've got a good grasp on my stance about the tough, merciless nature of business and of life in general, you'll understand why I chose to hark back to the past for wisdom from ancient warriors. Allow me to introduce to you the men who did competition best. These hardy warriors of the ancient world are the ultimate champions and their ability to see the world for what it really is allowed them to build empires, make millions and make history.

Luckily, they left behind them tales of their viewpoints, strategies and conquests, meaning that you can use their same pathways to gain your own success today!

Let's get started!

Chapter 1: Genghis Khan: What a Modern-Day Business Warrior Can Learn From the Greatest Conqueror of All Time: Part 1

Overcoming Adversity and Turning Challenges Into Lessons

In around 1162, Genghis Khan was born in a little-known corner of the remote Khentii Mountains of Mongolia. Over the course of his life, this man would become the greatest conqueror and most feared warrior ever known. Genghis' father was a minor noble and as a result, Genghis grew up with a certain amount of power and privilege.

However, when he was just 9 years old, Genghis' father was killed by the enemy Tatar tribe, leaving him, his siblings, and his mother in a vulnerable position. Though he was still young, Genghis tried to take up his father's position as a leader but members of the tribe refused to be led by him. They abandoned his mother and Genghis and his siblings instantly saw their lives change from one of privilege, power and protection to one of poverty, competition and fear. Many scholars believe that this event was a major turning point for the young Genghis. When he was faced with adversity and saw the world for what it really is- a fight for resources, survival and opportunity, he began to transform from a young, sheltered chieftain's son into a ruthless, tough-minded warrior.

While still very young, Genghis began to take care of his family, going out to hunt and scavenge in the wilderness in order to provide food for his mother and siblings. This mental toughness marked his evolution from a victim of his circumstances into a champion. As Genghis grew, his mother taught him to understand the stark reality of Mongolian tribal alliances where betrayal, revenge, capture and war where facts of daily life and this doubtless played a huge role in helping him to view the world without needing to sugar-coat it.

When he was in his early twenties, Genghis was kidnapped by people who had once been allies of his family and after managing to escape, his evolution into a full-grown warrior was complete. He now knew that without power and protection, others could abandon you, as his tribe had done to he and his mother, others could leave you without resources and if you were in an especially weak position, others could even attack and enslave you. Equipped with this view of the difficult, dangerous and competitive world around him, Genghis made a powerful decision: He would never again be a **victim**. Instead, he would become a **warrior**. It wasn't long before he used this decision and the many lessons that his painful experiences had taught him to form a force and to begin to amass power and support for himself.

How can you use this life-changing strategy in your own business and life? You must be able to own your experiences. Everyone has gone through difficulties and anyone who has suffered at all, in any way, has the ability to not only survive but to thrive. If you've ever lost a business you've worked incredibly hard to build or lost out on a promotion that you've been striving to gain for years, it's easy to take the victim route. It's amazing how inviting and almost addictive self-pity can be. And the reason that it feels so good is that it **DOESN'T REQUIRE YOU TO CHANGE!** Self-pity and viewing your experience as an enormous insurmountable challenge is attractive to so many people because it reinforces your own beliefs- "You're right and "they're" wrong", "You've been cheated out of what was rightfully yours", "You did everything perfectly and somehow, you just didn't get the results you wanted." All of these statements make it easy for you to sit back and avoid examining yourself. You can simply put the blame on anyone or anything else and keep on living, working, and thinking as you always have.

The difference between that kind of behavior and the reaction of a business warrior is this: A business warrior will feel just as frustrated, angry and disappointed as anyone else when things don't work out BUT, a warrior will funnel these emotions into useful action. Business warriors constantly examine their strategies and their behavior to look for ways to improve themselves. When challenges occur, they use them as an opportunity to test their strength and to "challenge-proof" their minds, habits and businesses in the future. Like Genghis Khan, they learn from every difficulty and they don't allow disappointment to cloud their vision.

One business leader I know went through losing his position as the head of his company due to a hostile takeover from a rival. He went through the gamut of emotions and struggled to keep going. At one point, he was even hospitalized for high blood pressure and depression. It seemed that his brilliant career and the rags-to-riches life story he was so proud of had ended in utter failure.

No one believed that he could recover from his losses, but in the end, that same warrior spirit that helped him build his business in the first place just wouldn't die out. He returned to work and formed a new, smaller, but almost equally successful company, **from the ground up**.

What drove him? According to him, it was the realization that he had failed to see the world around him for what it was and the determination to never make that same mistake again. His new company was built with iron-clad measures to ensure that he never loses control and his new mindset is prepared to see his weaknesses and fix them, before his competitors can exploit them. **Don't let victimization make you a victim**. When you refuse to remain subjugated by a challenge, when you come back stronger, time after time- that's when you know you've reached true **business warrior status.**

Playing a Zero-Sum Game:

Genghis foresaw that resources would become scarcer as the Mongol population increased and with the kind of clear-minded understanding that existed in the ancient world, he decided that to survive and thrive, his forces would have to control the territories that surrounded them.

Genghis achieved this through adopting a zero-sum mindset. He knew that for him to win, his adversaries must lose and equally, that if his adversaries won, it would mean disaster for him and his people. When business leaders today don't adopt this mindset, it ends up causing failure. The fact is, in any marketplace, no matter how abundant the opportunities or resources may seem to be, all resources are in fact, limited.

To be a true business warrior, you have to ignore the "win-win" strategies that we are taught to believe these days. Whether they are rival businesses or a group of colleagues vying for the same promotion, there simply is no way that all competitors can achieve what they want and benefit equally. That's a fairytale that we in the modern era have lulled ourselves to sleep with. The truth is that, to survive you must quickly and decisively claim your share of the benefits before someone else manages to claim them. This may mean working longer hours, putting in more effort than all of your competitors and most importantly, seeking strategic ways to overpower and outshine the competition. Don't get me wrong, winning at a zero-sum game is hard work but it is far better than the alternative of losing.

How can you adopt this mindset in your business activities? First, be honest with yourself about the nature of the situation you are in. Perhaps you work in a company that pushes collaboration and teamwork. That's great. Teamwork has its place and can be excellent for spurring innovation and growth. But here's the kicker. Although you should always appear cooperative and willing to work with others in your "team", don't forget that in reality, you are actually a team of one-yourself. Savvy business people know that working with others and trusting others are two completely different things.

Even in a team setting, you should always be looking for ways to standout in the crowd and to seize more power for yourself. If you think the other members of your team aren't doing the same thing, you're wrong. Human nature is essentially selfish and we are all lone wolves when it comes to seeking and seizing our prey. Genghis Khan learned this the hard way when he made an oath with Jamukha, one of his closest childhood friends. Although Jamukha and Genghis were part of the same force and even became "blood-brothers" Jamukha still betrayed Genghis in a bid to secure power for himself. Eventually, Genghis had to fight and decisively defeat his own childhood friend.

This led Genghis to understanding that even when you are the leader of a large team, in reality, it is always every man for himself. From then on Genghis Khan had many partners and companions during his numerous campaigns, but he always saw himself as a one-man army and led his life with a healthy suspicion of the motives of others. He once famously said: "<u>Remember, you have no companions but your own shadow.</u>"

Although life presents us with many situations in which we must collaborate with others, we can only achieve true success when we realize that even in the most tightly knit units, each warrior must fight his own battle.

Genghis Khan believed in self-reliance and cautioned against relying on others above oneself. He said: "No friend is better than your own wise heart! Although there are many things you can rely on, no one is more reliable than yourself. Although many people can be your helper, no one should be closer to you than your own consciousness. Although there are many things you should cherish, no one is more valuable than your own life."

This is why I always caution the business people that I coach to keep their eyes open and their senses extra-sharp when dealing with partners, teammates and colleagues. Every situation, whether it is a team presentation or a merger, is an opportunity for you to secure the greater share for yourself and it's also an opportunity for your "teammates" to try to do the same for themselves.

Your first loyalty in any business situation must be to yourself. Understanding this simple fact will help you to ensure that those working with you do not win at your expense.

Chapter 2: Genghis Khan: What a Modern-Day Business Warrior Can Learn From the Greatest Conqueror of All Time: Part 2

"If you're afraid - don't do it, - if you're doing it - don't be afraid!"

-Genghis Khan

Honing Your Strength:

It's said that as a young child, Genghis Khan used to test his speed and strength by filling his mouth with water and then running up and back down a mountain. He practiced doing this continually until at some point, he was actually able to run up and down the mountain fast enough to be able to spit out the entire mouthful. In this popular tale, we can find an important lesson. The true business warrior never stops training. Genghis Khan could easily have thought to himself "Look, I'm reasonably fit. I ride, I hunt. I can even race up and down mountains.

There's no need to up the ante by testing myself with a mouthful of water." But he recognized this: Today's challenges may have been won but tomorrow's challenges still await. What worked yesterday may not be enough to get you by in the future. If you ever become too comfortable with your victories, remember that there is always room for improvement and that somewhere, someone is working on surpassing you at this very moment.

In business, today's success story can very quickly become tomorrow's old news. If you're not constantly updating your offerings and reinforcing your strengths, it won't be long before some new upstart reaches and then overtakes you. Consider this: Main streets all over the country are littered with the remains of traditional businesses that failed to keep up with the killer pace of modern-day commerce. We all know of a popular bakery or restaurant that never had problems staying full and busy until one day, a newer, sleeker, more customer-oriented rival opened down the street from them.

Instead of changing to adopt some of the successful methods of their newer rivals, these businesses often stay stuck in their ways, believing that "what has always worked, will always work". Unfortunately that just isn't the case and the more we cling to the belief that we're good enough as we are and need no improvement, the more likely we are to fail the minute that we're faced with a new challenge. Whatever your strengths are, don't grow complacent. Keep learning from others who are at an even higher level than you. Take courses, get real-world practice and never stop moving. Genghis Khan understood that if you're not moving forward, you're actually moving backwards.

Begin With the End in Mind:

Genghis Khan held the ability to follow through with a planned course of action to be one of the highest skills a person could possess. He believed that "The merit in an action lies in finishing it to the end." Many of us are trapped in fruitless cycles of doing a little bit here and little bit there. This is particularly true for those of us who are serial entrepreneurs. It's incredibly easy to get caught up in thinking that we're doing a great deal of work, when in reality we may just be spinning our wheels. Are your daily actions helping you to close the gap between where you want to be financially and where you are or are they merely keeping you busy?

In his lifetime, Genghis Khan was able to conquer close to 12 million square miles of territory, a feat that no single human has ever been able to match. He did this in the space of only 40 years and the key to his astounding success may stem from his ability to achieve set goals in a methodical way. He didn't simply set out on his horse. He knew from a very young age that he wanted to be the conqueror of many lands and he began his campaign with this end in mind. Historians who examine his maneuvers today all agree that each move required a massive amount of detailed planning. Selecting his men, working out the logistics of feeding them and their horses, mapping out routes, deciding who to build alliances with and so much more- all of these things were managed through Genghis Khan's affinity for planning and his ability to stay committed and on-task.

When it comes to making money, planning is EVERYTHING. You probably have heard stories about people who started companies on a whim and a dream and managed to become overnight millionaires, without ever putting in a moment of planning -these stories are for the most part, urban legends. Every business leader worth the title is, or has learned to be, a meticulous planner. Studies have shown time and time again that placing your goals on paper and then working to map the road from your current financial situation all the way to your desired destination can improve business performance by 30 to 50%.

Many of the great business success stories of our time were built with a long term mindset. Warren

Buffet, for example, has always been an investor with his eye firmly on the long term payoff, rather than the quick buck. His slow and steady financial planning has reaped massive rewards that withstood the boom and bust of several economic downturns and his unswerving focus on the future has made his company, Berkshire Hathaway, a true champion among all multi-national conglomerate holding companies.

This isn't something you can avoid. You may have been a nonchalant and plan-free person in the past but here's my question to you: Has this attitude gotten you to where you want to be? Or has it actually hindered your progress? Be honest with yourself and you'll see just how many opportunities may have been missed due to the lack of both a vision and clearly outlined steps to achieving it.

If you're like the average adult, you probably spend a total of 3-4 hours a month analyzing your finances and planning your next steps. For the majority of people, these 3-4 hours are most probably spent dealing with bills and wondering how to cover all expenses. By contrast, the wealthy spend at least 20 to 25 hours monthly on examining their finances, setting up short term plans and making sure that they are on the road to achieving previously set long term goals.

Just think about all of the time, effort and energy you devote to many other things and you'll quickly see that at least some of this should be diverted to analyzing your current financial state and planning out your financial future. The more familiar you become with every part of your moneymaking and money-spending process, the less likely you'll be to make silly decisions, lose sight of your goals or spend mindlessly. Think of your finances as your force and see yourself as a young Genghis Khan, starting from the bottom and carefully crafting and carrying out strategies to become more than what you are. While everyone's financial journey is different, money spent on a consultation with a reputable financial planner is money well-spent. You'll be able to have your money clearly set out for you: How much you're making versus how much you need to be making to get where you would like to be, how many years that will take, what factors stand in your way, how to avoid or pay off debts and so much more can be covered in these consultations. You can never totally leave the planning to an outsider, just as a leader can't ever fully outsource his leadership duties, but a professional can assist you in the same way that Genghis Khan's great deputies were able to help him see and build his dream.

You may think that your daily grind is over the minute the working day ends but in all actuality, you're still in the midst of a struggle during your downtime. Numerous concerns and distractions can come in and cloud your clear vision, leaving you unable to focus on the goals you've set for yourself. Genghis Khan kept himself focused on his vision by continually remaining a horseman, someone constantly in-touch and familiar with the smallest details of his empire's running. By doing so, he never lost sight of his target and was able to achieve with a single-mindedness that terrified his foes and secured his empire. You can use these tactics for yourself, by "keeping your mind on your money", as they say.

20 hours a month (or 5 hours a week) and a small investment in a meeting with a good financial planner are practical sacrifices that can help you to achieve the financial independence that you want. However you prefer to plan, do it. Make sure you are moving towards your goals every single day.

Be Fast and Flexible:

When Genghis Khan and his hordes of horsemen burst onto the scene, the world was astonished. The ancient civilizations he swept through had never seen anything like the tightly coordinated, swift and self-sufficient fleets of horsemen and were completely baffled by this new ultra-fast form of dominance.

The Mongols would arguably never have changed the history of the world in the way they did if it hadn't been for their famed horsemanship and their ability to quickly change to suit a new situation. Being a Mongol warrior was all about practicing agility and speed. Mongol horsemen trained since childhood to be excellent mounted archers. They learned how to send devastatingly accurate arrows from the saddle of a racing horse, which helped them to destroy fleeing opponents as they chased them. They were also able to use their bows and arrows while riding backwards on their horses or even hanging off the edge of their saddles, if need be.

For many years, size and a long history of success were the most important advantages a business could have. If you were big and established, you were automatically unassailable. These days, it's a totally different story. We've seen it in all arenas of business. There are massive companies being made irrelevant by groups of young kids who created innovative solutions that these companies couldn't. There are traditional publishing houses going under because savvy entrepreneurs are making a killing in the eBook business, and there are media companies that don't have half the following of some bloggers and YouTube stars. Why?

All of the established businesses are too big. You've heard the phrase "too big to fail", but these days it's more like "too big to succeed". Many larger, older businesses are calcified. They can't change their long-held ways of dealing with customers, creating products or advertising, so they end up becoming dinosaurs. In this day and age, everything moves at lightning speed and if you're not moving with the tide, you're getting crushed.

In this kind of environment, it's the lone entrepreneur, the owner of a small or medium-sized business, the serial startup creator, who can benefit the most. If that's you, your advantage is in your small size and your speed.

I'll give you an example: Elise, an entrepreneur friend of mine, had previously worked for a mid-range cosmetics firm. She'd repeatedly heard customers complain about the lack of variety in shades and the difficult application of some of the products, as well as the inflated price points but management refused to consider her suggested changes. When Elise left the company, she used her savings to work with experts to create a small, simple line of makeup that answered the concerns that customers had brought up over and over again, while keeping price points low. And with some careful advertising, Elise was able to outsell the company she'd previously worked for in one area of the market.

It's that simple. Anyone with the ability to listen to customers, to really understand what people want and what gets under their skin, can easily take on a larger business opponent and win. In Elise's case, her former employers had an outdated and rigid management structure that prevented them from making, or even suggesting, changes to the higher ups. No one was listening to the customer feedback. No one was looking at new trends or considering the budgets of their buyers-no one except for Elise. If she had hesitated, had waited for a better time, then someone else would have eventually come to the same realizations as she had and would have created the products themselves. Instead, she took her savings and her knowledge and she made her move.

If you're worried that your small size prevents you from being competitive, this is your time. Technology has leveled the playing field. Your job is to work on spotting the needs, the gaps, the customer concerns before the big guys, and thinking of ways to address them. If you train yourself to move quickly, to adapt your model or solution in times of change, you'll be golden.

Think about this: Genghis Khan's hordes were extremely skilled at attacking on horseback. After all, it was what they had been born and bred to do. And for the most part, it worked against opponents brilliantly. But when it came to taking the well-defended, fully walled cities of some Persian or Chinese regions, their horsemanship had little value. So they changed their tactics. They learned from their new situation and instead adopted new techniques, including flooding towns with rerouted streams, isolating the towns to cause hunger and submission and even tossing large stones over the walls, using a catapult. With these new techniques, they were able to win. The lesson is clear: When situations change, adapt as quickly and fearlessly to the new circumstances as possible. If you do, you can rip victory out of the hands of your competitors. If you don't, someone else will come along and take your business victory from you.

The tactics and lessons outlined above are some of the secrets behind Genghis Khan's amazing success. Using them, this abandoned young man from the remote Mongolian steppes was able to conquer more lands and people in just 25 years than the entire Roman Empire managed to do in 400 years of power. Imagine what these techniques could do for you and your business!

Chapter 3: The Power of Perception: Building Your Own Intimidating Personal Brand, Part 1

"All of us need to understand the importance of branding. We are CEOs of our own companies: Me Inc. To be in business today, our most important job is to be head marketer for the brand called You."

– Tom Peters, writer on business management practices

When Genghis Khan and his hordes attacked a large territory, they would sometimes be outnumbered by their opponents. Did that mean certain defeat? Absolutely not. You see, Genghis Khan understood something that very often makes the difference between loss and victory: Perception.

It doesn't matter what your numbers **actually are**. It only matters how high your opponent can be made to **believe they are**.

When the Mongol army approached a massive army, Genghis Khan and his generals would order that each unit be split up into at least 3 smaller groupings. These groups would then attempt to come upon their opponents by surprise, seeming to appear out of thin air and shocking their opponents by what would seem like their endless numbers.

At night, when they Mongols camped out close to their opponents, they would create the perception of an enormous camp full of large amounts of soldiers by having every single man light 5-10 fires each. When their opponents looked out into the darkness, they would see a never-ending expanse of campfires, making them think that the camped Mongol forces were much larger than they really were.

Genghis Khan came up with many ways of terrifying opponents into believing that his forces were far superior, but one of the most ingenious of his tactics was the effect of "clouds of fury". If you've ever seen films or documentaries about Genghis Khan and his men, you'll likely see depictions of them charging down hillsides with enormous clouds of dust being churned up behind their horses. This isn't just fancy Hollywood imagery. It's a fact. But in reality, this was just a "sleight of hand" technique used by the great Khan to trick his enemies. He ordered that all horsemen under his command had to tie a grouping of tree branches behind their horses as they attacked. The forces would then move in a strategic pattern that allowed the branches to drag on the ground and stir up clouds of dust and sand. When each of these clouds rose behind the riders, they formed one gigantic cloud of dust and sand that made it appear that thousands upon thousands of riders were charging against a territory. The inhabitants of the attacked territory would fail to realize that they actually outnumbered the Khan's men and would instead be so terrified by the clouds and perceived size of the force that they abandoned their safe cities and escaped out into the fields, making themselves easy targets.

If they had examined the Khan's forces systematically, they would have quickly noticed that their own men were numerically superior. This simple realization would have allowed them to stay, fight and most probably, defeat the Mongol forces. But they couldn't. Why? **They were paralyzed by the power of perception.**

When it comes to the battle for greater business share, more respect and ultimately more power, perception is your most important weapon. It will be there when you have no wealth, no experience and no portfolio and can be used to totally turn your position around. Equally, after gaining a greater amount of financial stability, you can still use perception's power to gain even more.

If you take little else to heart in this book, please take this section seriously. Once you've harnessed the power of perception and used it successfully in even one instance, you'll instantly see all of the other areas of your life that could benefit from this same tool.

The most effective way to get into the heads of those you need to influence and leave them with the perception that you are powerful, strong, skilled and important is to control your image. We all know that people form an opinion of someone within seconds of seeing them, but did you know that people actually decide whether you are successful or not within as little as 5 seconds? And as we know, first impressions may be softened or shifted slightly but they can rarely be completely changed.

This means that, no matter how experienced, skilled or competent you are on paper, it all counts for very little if you aren't allowing yourself to be perceived positively. This chapter is all about the steps you can take today to make sure that you're getting the right message across and that people view you the way you need them to, for greater success.

Keeping Up Appearances:

If there's one thing I can't abide, it's the number of supposed "consultants" out there who will tell you that your appearance doesn't matter at all. They claim that people make business decisions based on far more than something as superficial as looks. They are lying and unfortunately, these kinds of lies can make someone's climb to the top a lot more arduous and lengthy than it needs to be.

Just think about it: What's a business decision but a choice about where or how to spend resources? When you go to a store and choose among countless varieties of the same product, doesn't eye-catching packaging play a role in your final decision? That's why corporations spend millions of dollars on branding and testing different types of packaging- they know what we all know deep down, looks matter.

Now, does this mean that business success is the sole domain of super-models? Of course not. It's all about projecting *power* and a sense of *quality*, rather than just physical beauty.

So how do we achieve this image? Let's take a look at some ways in the following section. Some changes are so simple and instinctive that you'll have no problem adopting them, while others may require more effort. Regardless, all come together to guarantee a powerful presence that your business allies, foes and targets are certain to perceive.

Chapter 4: The Appearance of Power: Building Your Own Intimidating Personal Brand, Part 2

"...The appearance of power is therefore almost as important as the reality of it. In fact, the appearance is frequently its essential reality."

-Henry Kissinger, US politician

Clothes Don't Make the Man, But They Can Help to Make the Deal: How to Equip Yourself For Business Battle

We notice what others wear. If you were asked to describe the person in front of you at Starbucks this morning, you would likely spend time explaining the color and shape of the person's outfit. Clothes are "social signifiers", those little hints that tell us what class and status a person is likely to occupy and to pretend that what we wear doesn't matter is to fool ourselves and miss a great opportunity.

According to Harvard Business School professor Amy Cuddy, people answer 2 questions, within moments of meeting you:

Can I trust this person? Can I respect this person?

Because we can't write our personalities on our faces, clothing offers a major clue. Are you working towards partnering with top business leaders? Do you want to attract top-flight investors to your projects? People are far more likely to handover money, power and responsibility to those who look like they already have those things. In the same way, people are more likely to accord respect to those who appear to be used to receiving respect from others and look like they hold themselves in high esteem.

In order to benefit from these common prejudices, you've got to look like you care about yourself.

Carelessly chosen and put together clothing, bitten nails, an unkempt hairstyle and a complexion that shows you haven't put any work into it are just some of the signals that will convince others that you deserve neither respect nor trust. So what kind of clothing sends the right message? While every niche, workplace and market is different, there are some things that work across the board.

* Look for Quality Fabrics: Too often, people focus on trendiness. Wearing the hot new color or the most popular silhouettes shouldn't distract you from one of the most noticeable factors in your look. How many times have you spotted a well-dressed person from afar, only to draw near and realize that cheap fabrics and accessories have marred their look? We live in a "fast-fashion" era and while this affords us a lot of choice, it doesn't always bode well for quality. You need to become an expert in quality. Even if you're not particularly interested in fashion, this is essential to remember. I often advise young people going out to secure funding for their innovations and I stress this point:

Steer clear of all clothing that is made up of more than 20% synthetic material. Anything above that and the clothing will practically announce its cheapness from a mile away.

*Swap Out Plastic Buttons: This is the most common mistake and one that is so unnecessary. Plastic buttons can easily be replaced with a good set of mother of pearl, horn or other quality buttons and this one simple move will instantly lift your look. People notice the details. Get them right and the rest will fall into place.

* For Men, Stay Away From Suits with Low Arm Holes and Bubbly Shoulders: There are plenty of suits that, while inexpensive, look like a million bucks. On the other hand, suits that feature low armholes will give you a boxy, "winged" look and suits that bubble up around the shoulders are a sure sign of low-quality. That's because suits that are factory produced feature cut and paste designs that leave armholes and shoulders looking too large and too low. Look for clean lines across the shoulders and high armholes, to create a sharp impression.

*For Women, Avoid Tops and Dresses Featuring Tiny, Complicated Patterns: A bold print can announce your style and confidence to the world but you'll want to stay away from fussy patterns on cheaper items. This is because they rarely match up to the quality of prints on expensive pieces. They can tend to look faded or skewed and just have an overall "less-than-top drawer" look. If you can't clearly identify the print on an outfit from across the room, don't buy it. Stick to blocks of color for items that are cheaper and splurge on pricier items for prints, to always communicate a polished, wealthy image.

*Baggy Fits Don't Work: Whether for males or females, nothing looks less pulled together and sharp than baggy, ill-fitting clothing. It doesn't matter what size, shape or height you are, being well-dressed hinges heavily on choosing clothing that outlines your shape, not swallows it. Many of us feel uncomfortable with body conscious clothing, but while skin-tight is not an appropriate option, a good close fit is a great way to announce your confidence and comfort with yourself. In addition, high quality clothing is often cut to fit the body much more closely than mass-produced items, marking you out as a discerning and well-dressed person.

*Invest In The Important Things: While well-chosen reasonably priced clothing can easily look expensive and stylish, the same can't be said for footwear and timepieces. This is why people who want to quickly gauge a person's wealth and status will immediately scope out these two items first. So while it may be a burden on the budget, invest in some good pairs of leather shoes and a quality watch. These items are a form of ID. Wealthy people tend to check for these pieces in order to find out if you're "part of the club."

Male or female, young or old, long-time entrepreneur or hopeful upstart, these two items will anchor your look, announce your standing in the business world and will open doors for you that you didn't even realize existed.

***Don't Follow the Group. Lead the Group:** What's the first thing you think of when you imagine an outfit for an upscale event or important meeting? Do you imagine a dark colored suit or a quiet black dress? This mistake pertains to women most of all because there's a prevalent myth that color and style equals overly feminine or unprofessional. Forget that. Some of the most powerful business people in the world wear bold shades, for the express purpose of standing out from the crowd. If you walk into a function where everyone is in "tasteful black" and you've had the same idea, how on earth are you going to make an impression? Those who follow the "when in doubt, wear black" rule are very frequently those who are not in the know. Don't err on the side of caution with your style. Dress for the job or career you want by having the guts to be stylish. For many years, I've had the chance to observe people as they made their way up the career ladder and I've noticed that those who follow the group sartorially always remain just another member of the group. This is a mistake. You always want to appear bigger, stronger, better than your opponents. Blending in usually leads to disappearing.

On the other hand, those who dress a little better than the group tend to end up leading. It's all about intimidation, in the end. While you needn't look fashion-obsessed, when you do choose to dress better than those around you, you announce self-love, assurance and even strength. People respond to this display of strength by offering you respect, attention and opportunity. When you dress well and take care of your appearance, others give you what you want because they believe you already have it.

Never forget, when it comes to the battle of succeeding in business-perception is power. Genghis Khan, with his tactics to make his forces appear more numerous than they really were knew it, every business warrior who started from the bottom and hustled and bluffed all the way to the top knew it and now, so do you.

Chapter 5: Learning From Attila the Hun: Three Critical Lessons to Elevate Your Business Battle Skills Instantly

"What business strategy is all about-what distinguishes it from all other kinds of business planning-is, in a word, competitive advantage. Without competitors there would be no need for strategy, for the sole purpose of strategic planning is to enable the company to gain, as efficiently as possible, a sustainable edge over its competitors."

- Kenichi Ohmae, organizational theorist, management consultant and author

There are countless leadership and business books that draw on the examples and prowess of noble historical figures and there's a prejudice against learning from the notorious as well as the famous. But I've decided to deviate from this tradition because if there's one thing that we all come to understand eventually, it's that every single person who has achieved a challenging goal offers us invaluable knowledge. With that in mind, I've decided to delve into the brutal history of a man known for his cruelty, because bad or good, he managed to change the face of the world and left behind him some important lessons that we can use in business strategy.

Born in 406, in a little known corner of the Roman Empire called Pannonia, Attila the Hun would become notorious as the man who devastated the Roman Empire and conquered immense parts of Europe. From ascending to the throne of a relatively obscure and unimportant kingdom to gaining so much power that he was called "Flagellum Dei" the "Scourge of God", the path that Attila the Hun forged has become legendary for both its sheer ruthlessness and its efficacy.

Commit Completely or Fail Utterly:

Few traits are as vital for a business warrior as commitment to their goals. Unswerving determination eventually gives birth to rich rewards and this is brilliantly exemplified by the behavior of the young Attila. When Attila was a young man, he was the favored nephew of the Hun king Rugila. However, that didn't stop him from seeing how his uncle's policies were forcing the Hun nation into weakness and subjugation under the Roman Empire.

His anger and frustration at these policies, coupled with a fierce love for the Hun nation and his dreams of seeing it free made him an unpopular critic at court. His uncle the King sent him away to the Roman court, as part of a scheme that swapped Roman youth with the youth of subjugated courts, in what was touted as a sort of "cultural exchange program". In reality, he had been handed over by his uncle as a child-captive.

Once at the courts of the Roman Emperor Honorius, the 12 year old Attila was presented with all of the power, pomp and glory of the Empire. It was meant to overwhelm, impress and subdue the boy, while influencing him to want to mimic Roman ways. Other Hun child-captives sent with him were weaker and quickly succumbed to the luxuries of court life, but Attila was different. He rejected the extravagant customs, clothing and habits of the Romans and remained a true Hun at heart. He kept his nation at the forefront of his mind and although he was unable to escape his captivity, Attila used his time to further his goals. He listened and learned all he could about the Roman Empire. He studied the details of Roman policies, of their forces, their plans and their diplomatic tactics. Without knowing it, the Romans were thoroughly instructing their future opponent.

Attila would grow up to use every detail he had learned against the Roman Empire, turning the tables of power and decisively defeating his former captors. It was this long term thinking and ability to remain absolutely 100% committed to his goal that brought Attila ultimate success and this is the same trait that can completely turn your life story around, starting from this very moment. Do you have a business idea that you are convinced will work? Are you stuck in the planning stages and losing hope because the funds to make your plan a reality simply aren't there yet? Then you are exactly where so many would-be entrepreneurs have been. And this may actually be the most crucial stage of your future success.

Ask yourself one question: Am I committed? Commitment stands for very little these days and we all seem to have the attention spans of gnats, but that kind of lack of long term thinking spells disaster for business. If you're truly committed to your business, you can wait while the slow, painstaking and often, seemingly impossible stages pass. You can wait and work towards you goal in thousands of invisible ways, just as Attila secretly kept the dream of a strong Hun nation in his heart, while he gathered, bit by bit, the information he needed to make his dream a fact. When your competitors have given up, packed up and gone home, you have to be there, lurking, waiting for the final victory. Whether this means slow and excruciating financial planning and saving, setting aside time after work every day to work towards your business goals or gathering information about your market and future competitors, even when all you have is a hope and a plan- do it. Don't fall down at the first and most crucial step. Commit to your goals absolutely. That's the warrior way and it's the ONLY way to achieve meaningful business success.

Unify to Win:

One of the most important accomplishments of Attila the Hun was his unification of the dispersed and weakened tribes of the Hun kingdom. Bringing these peoples together, he was able to form a strong, centrally-ruled nation that was then able to wreak havoc on nations and territories far better armed and technologically advanced than they were. You can use this tactic to your advantage as well. Are you a family-run business? Nix any squabbles and think of yourselves as one impenetrable unit, to win in a way that larger, less unified businesses can't.

Are you running a business that suffers from a lack of strong teamwork? Whip your group into shape with activities that bring everyone together and reward unity while you punish disloyalty and dissonance within the group. Attila was known for his loyalty to his men and to the Hun nation. He punished any attempts to destroy unity severely and you will have to do the same. While, like all wise leaders, he trusted no one fully, he did know that he had to lead by example and appearing to trust his forces and people implicitly taught others in the group that disloyalty had no place.

If one member of your team is continually breaking down the bonds that hold you all together, it's time to remove that person.

Be the Barbarian at the Gate:

Sometimes, there's nothing more powerful than being an outsider. In business, so many spend their time socializing, hob-knobbing, gossiping, learning the pervasive lingo and touting the accepted new trends in an effort to be thought of as "in". What if you turned this idea upside down and proudly flaunted your outsider status?

This is exactly what Attila did. During his youth and conquests, the Roman Empire was considered the height of sophistication and knowledge. The Huns and other barbarian tribes were thought of as extremely primitive, backwards and incapable. As a result they were engaged in busily striving to be regarded as civilized by adopting the ways and practices of the Romans.

Attila however, chose a different path. He proclaimed the excessive luxuries of Rome to be disgusting and destructive. He called on barbarian tribes to return to their nomadic, simple and heroic traditions. Once he taught his people to march to the beat of their own unique drum, he was able to use their inherent strengths against the superior power of the Roman Empire. What is your unique strength? What sets you apart from the crowd? Rather than viewing your difference as a weakness, why not make it your business's overpowering strength?

I know of one family-run restaurant that didn't have the funds to secure a liquor license after opening. This eatery was located in a very lively, nightlife-heavy neighborhood and as a result, suffered because it couldn't cater to a large slice of clientele.

In the end, instead of trying to match the hip vibe of the establishments around it, this place rebranded itself in order to play up its family-friendly image. This resulted in massive interest from diners who were more interested in having a nice meal with their kids than going to a buzzing, club-like restaurant. This restaurant managed to capitalize on its difference by proudly being the "barbarian at the gate". So what can you do with your disadvantage?

If you're smaller than your competitors, use your small size and speed to nimbly outpace their business's red tape. If you're considered an outsider, brand your rebel image and appeal to consumers who want a different and less conventional or less obviously contrived product or experience.

For every perceived weakness, there are literally dozens of ways to flip it into a strong point so unique that your competitors can't match it. Go on, unleash your inner barbarian and start reaping the business rewards today.

Chapter 6: The Gladiator: How to Dominate Any Arena You Enter

"What you are speaks so loudly I cannot hear a word you say."

- Ralph Waldo Emerson

Imagine a gladiator standing in the darkened wings of a tunnel, waiting to enter the arena. He would be aware that this next battle could decide his final fate- victory or defeat, life or death. He would feel the weight of commanding hands, pushing him out into the harsh sunlight of the dusty arena, into the roar of the blood-thirsty crowd eagerly awaiting his defeat and even though he would be in chains, blinded by the sudden sunlight and confused by the noise- he would have to stand strong. Throwing back his shoulders, lifting his head, raising himself to his full height and projecting all of the power, the confidence and strength that he could muster- the gladiator would have no choice but to ignore the heart-pounding fear he most likely felt and to do all of these things.

Why?

Because to show any fear, any weakness, doubt or anxiety at all would be to seal his fate and assure his defeat, destruction, and death. The roaring crowds would immediately recognize any hesitation and would mock and distract him. Whether man or animal, his opponent, standing on the other end of the arena would also instantly pickup on the scent of human fear and would be emboldened to attack with greater ferocity. So the gladiator would swallow his fear, call up his pride and put all of his strength into dominating the arena with his persona. His life depended on it.

So what connects us to the gladiator's experience? We may not realize it, but at every stage of our lives, our success and survival all hinge on being able to project an image of confidence and strength.

People are no different from any other creatures when it comes to sensing fear in others. Those who project an image of fear, self-doubt and lack of confidence cause us to doubt, mistrust and even dislike them, almost instantly.

Every single one of us is a gladiator in our own right and our arenas are our workplaces, our business markets and our social circles.

Even if you aren't fighting to the death in a gory battle, surrounded by jeering crowds watching your every move, make no mistake-every single time you enter a boardroom, an office or an event, you are being judged. And good or bad, that judgment will follow you in any future dealings with the people you've met.

In life, first impressions count. In business, they count for even more.

Contrary to popular myth, people don't do business with businesses. They do business with people. And very often, the way people "feel" about you will override facts on paper such as history of success, net worth or level of knowledge. You'll hear business people talking about how they always "listen to their gut" when hiring employees or selecting partners to do business with and that's what this chapter is all about: Speaking not to the minds of people but directly to their guts and sending out one message, loud and clear- that you are powerful.

The only real way to viscerally affect others is to make an indelible first impression. Let's take a look at how best to achieve this every time you enter a room.

Don't Be Late: This is perhaps the simplest change you can make but it creates a huge difference in how you're perceived. Many people think that arriving late is a sign that you're busy, important, that you've got things to do. Trust me, it's not a good look. The reason why lateness backfires is that it sends a very clear signal to those waiting for you- you are not a person of your word. You may think punctuality is essential because it shows that you respect others.

The truth is that it actually shows that you respect yourself. People who hold themselves in high esteem don't make promises they can't keep, not because they don't want to let others down but because they don't make a habit of letting themselves down. True leaders understand that their word is their bond. This is how they control their message.

A commitment to keeping your promises when it comes to smaller details like time let's people know that you're committed to yourself, to your honor and that you give your words value. It's really that simple.

Enter Boldly: Once you've arrived, don't make the mistake of making an "unassuming entrance". I've actually seen attendees at conferences and other events wait until eyes would be turned away from the door, before making an entrance. They feel that coming in when others might "notice them" could seem self-important or attention-seeking. Let me clarify one thing right here- leaders are beyond attention. We've all seen people who seem not to even notice that every single eye in the room is on them. These people enter a room in the same, bold, confident way whether it's a star-studded gala, a boardroom packed with their superiors or a McDonalds. They've already come to the point where they've made absolute peace with who they are. They know themselves deeply, they respect themselves and it shows. Wherever you are, walk in like you belong there. I'm sure you've seen people who seem to physically shrink when entering a lavish restaurant, a designer store or the lobby of a 5 star hotel. Why? Internally and probably quite unconsciously, they are measuring themselves against their surroundings and saying "Nope, I don't match up. This is too good for me." This kind of thinking can be very hard to escape because it's rooted in a belief. If this is a problem for you, first, change the belief. Then you'll be able to change the behavior.

 If you're used to internally telling yourself that you don't belong in certain places, turn this statement on its head. Instead, minutes before stepping into a room, tell yourself to walk in as though you owned the place. Not figuratively-literally. Enter as though you've entered that same room a thousand times, as though you already know every detail of it. Save the close inspection of your surroundings for a time when others aren't watching you. Eagerly scoping out the room as you come in can make you appear as though you've never been in that type of environment and that, as a result, you're intimidated and awed. If you haven't managed to build a base of confidence yet, follow one of the biggest maxims of business: Fake it 'til you make it. Gladiators were, no doubt, truly terrified before entering the arena to do battle with deadly animals and lethal opponents, but they also recognized that to come in quaking in fear would be fatal.

Don't display your fears, doubts or insecurities to the world. The world is a cut-throat place and doesn't care about the finer points of your problems. Whether your lack of confidence stems from past bullying or you're struggling to manage your finances, the world is completely uninterested. It sees weakness and it sees strength. That's all. It punishes weakness and it rewards strength. You have to choose a side to stand on and assume your stance with complete conviction.

Remember that nobody truly knows the inner workings of your life, so even if you're going through a rough patch, it doesn't have to show. Each of us has the gift of being able to push away our problems and present a strong, bold and impenetrable exterior to the world when we need to.

Pay Attention to Your Pre-Game: This may not always be possible, particularly if you haven't had time to prepare, but when you know you'll be going somewhere especially important, take a little extra time with your pre-game.

- **Be Prepared:** Wherever you're headed, don't be ashamed to put in the time to research and prepare for it thoroughly. The internet is your friend. If you've been invited out to a new restaurant for a business dinner, Google it. Find out what diners wear, what the prices and menu are like and anything else that will help you arrive like you're in control. You may have that familiar voice in your head saying "Don't try too hard." Shut it down. True warriors never pass over any tactical advantage. With so much free and anonymously accessible information at your fingertips, you'd be foolish to go into any situation blind.

Multi-millionaire and Shark Tank Judge Kevin O'Leary once shared this anecdote about being ready: Kevin once received a great pitch from a clever salesman who was trying to license his exciting product to him. The only problem was- this smart salesman made a very silly mistake He didn't realize that Kevin O'Leary had actually just launched a competing product! Imagine how easily a little preparation and research could have prevented that sticky situation.

Knowing as much as possible about the environment you'll be navigating, the market you're selling to and the people you'll be dealing with not only provides you with valuable information, it also gives you an added sense of confidence. The more you know, the more you'll be able to plan your steps and say to yourself without doubt "You've got this." And guess what? It will show.

- **Looks:** While ancient warriors carefully applied war paint to surprise and paralyze their enemies with shock and awe, these days the method may be different, but appearance is no less important. Make sure you're regularly following a maintenance plan for your appearance, because a sudden grooming session can work wonders but the fact is, we can all tell when someone who's used to jeans is wearing a brand new suit for the first time. Grooming has got to be a habit for it to be effective at all. So before you walk into a room, just take a moment to be certain that you've followed the basic rules of good self-care: Are your shoes polished, your clothes wrinkle-free? Is your hair in place, your hands well-maintained and your breath fresh? Once you're set in this department, you're free to enter without doubt. People gauge you first on your appearance and if you've taken care of that, half the battle is already won.

Dominant Body Language:

If you ever had to identify a multi-millionaire out of a line-up of ordinary Joes, I guarantee you that it would be difficult to do so solely on the basis of clothing and accessories. In my line of work, I come across many high-net worth individuals and if I were to judge them based upon the estimated value of their clothing alone, I would likely never recognize their status. Because the business world is such a high-stakes, competitive arena, plenty of people work hard to put their best foot forward and you'll find that most are well-dressed, well-shod and have at least one statement piece that makes them look richer than they are. If you're picking a truly successful person out of a crowd of pretenders, clothing can give you a hint, but it isn't enough.

However, when it comes to how people hold themselves, it's a totally different story.

Several years ago, I was asked to speak at an employee's retreat for a newly successful tech company. Later, as I mingled with my audience, I noticed one particular young man across the room. He didn't stand out in any way that you could put your finger on: He was neither very tall nor well-built and was not flashily dressed. But there was something about him-a quiet confidence that showed in his great posture, his relaxed movements, the way he seemed to own the room. When he was introduced to me as the founder and CEO of the company, I instantly understood what it was that I had seen. It was the "millionaire effect." That's a term I've coined for the kind of assured, powerful and charismatic aura that seems to follow those who have been particularly successful in life. And while you may not have reached the financial stage that you want to yet, you can still harness this amazing effect to your advantage.

We communicate far more with our bodies and movements than we can ever say with words. When people catch our physical signals, they are far more likely to take them as true than they would be with spoken messages. That's why it's crucial to present body language that displays confidence.

Better known as power posturing, this type of body language explains quickly and clearly to anyone w you meet that you're a capable, self-assured and powerful person. Power posturing starts with excellent posture. If you're the kind of person who hunches, slumps forward or buries your head into your chest, you're causing your image immeasurable damage. Poor posture tells those who see you that you are passive, indecisive, uneasy, and unimportant.

All of these things can be summed up in one word- weak. When you enter a room and compress your body together, people instinctively view this as you trying to minimize the amount of space you take up for yourself , because YOU ARE LESS IMPORTANT THAN OTHERS. I've seen this time and time again, and unfortunately, women are often the biggest offenders when it comes to this kind of behavior. While it's certainly rude to monopolize more than your fair share of space in a crowded setting, going out of your way to appear small and accommodating isn't polite. It's dangerous. It makes you an instant victim. You might as well place a large target sign on your back, because that's how everyone will perceive you.

On the other hand, taking up space naturally presents you as a VIP. We're all highly attuned to social signs of importance and when you place your hands on your hips, broaden your shoulders or stand with your feet akimbo, you're basically silently telling everyone "I matter. I deserve more room than the average person." So what's the appropriate stance for a person seeking to project power?

Stand Tall:

Keep your head held high. This, above all, denotes importance. One effective trick is to take and hold a breath as you come into a place. This has the effect of forcing you to stand taller and as you slowly exhale, you're relaxing all of the muscles in your face, neck and shoulders.

Make sure that your shoulders don't ride up. This is a common mistake and it implies tension and anxiety. Instead, drop your shoulders and allow them to rest held back in a natural, low position.

When you stand, place your feet firmly on the ground and share your body weight equally between them.

Breathe from your gut. Shallow chest-led breathing will lead to tension in your shoulders neck and chest, lifting and stiffening them and making you look as though you're trying to look confident but are actually nervous.

Hold yourself from your center. Make your stomach muscles the basis of your posture and you won't have to worry about rising shoulders or a stiff neck.

Hold Your Head In a Dominant Way:

Surprisingly, one of the best ways to communicate dominance is to hold your head still. Anxious people, particularly those who are anxious to please, move their heads around as they communicate. They may swing their head from side to side as they seek approval from one and then another member of the group, or they may nervously jerk their heads up and down, trying to make a point or show that they agree with others. None of these things are a part of power posturing. Stillness of the head and a lack of over-animated facial expressions is one of the signifiers of the "millionaire effect" and can be seen in leaders. People who are comfortable in a situation and confident about their effect on others don't need to move around to seek approval or make points. They communicate calmly and with the full belief that they can gain and hold the attention of others without putting on a show.

Make Eye Contact:

There's a misunderstanding that the most powerful people in a room are the ones who focus only on themselves. That's a complete fallacy. Charisma shines through most when a person is confident, relaxed and happy with themselves, while also being interested in other people. People never remember anything about you as much as they remember *the way that you made them feel*.

The best and easiest way to connect with others and leave an excellent first impression is to look them in the eye as you speak with them. But making and maintaining eye contact properly is an art. The last thing you want to do is to stare into someone's eyes until they end up feeling uncomfortable. That's creepy, not charismatic. Make a point of occasionally focusing on and then gradually focusing away from the person's eyes. This is the most natural way to ensure that you're not locking your conversation partner into a scary staring contest.

Try this in small amounts and you'll start to notice a difference when you speak with others. They'll warm to you quickly, draw nearer to you, and want to confide in you. This is human nature. We are magnetically pulled towards the people who are both secure in themselves and interested in us. Lots of books will tell you that this is the only thing you'll ever need in order to attract and keep the attention of others. I wouldn't go that far. If you're not combining this eye contact technique with dominant body language and an assured manner, you'll simply seem like you're fawning over others.

They won't respect your interest because they'll feel that you are somehow in a subordinate position. Your eye contact will be perceived as a sign that you focus on others because you don't value yourself. That's obviously not what we want, so make sure that increased eye contact is always paired with the other techniques for showing off your assured, strong persona.

Extend a Firm Hand:

It may seem like a no-brainer but you'd be surprised by the number of people who still don't understand the importance of a firm handshake.

Extending a limp hand to others reads very, very negatively. One CEO told me that he doesn't do business with those who don't understand the value of a strong handshake. According to him, every person he's worked with who didn't shake hands with energy and firmness always ended up being a problem-avoider or a the kind of person who seeks the "easy way out" in every situation.

That's a whole lot of judgment based on a simple skill that you can improve in minutes. Don't go in trying to crush the person you're greeting but do put some pressure in that grip. It will make all the difference in the way you're perceived.

The moves outlined in this section may appear to be extremely easy, even intuitive. They are. But that doesn't mean that people actually remember to do them. Battles are won and lost on something as simple as perception. Don't fall into the trap that it's you MBA or your company's value that speaks for you. Business is not automated It's still carried out by people and it's a contact sport.

Come into any business situation ready to dominate, to make your presence and your strength felt. Build an image of self-worth and confidence and you'll find that others are much more likely to give you the attention, time and opportunities you need to get ahead.

Check out the next chapter to learn about some common habits that could secretly be destroying your strong image and ruining your winning edge.

Chapter 8: Nice Guys Don't Survive The Wilderness: Lessons From the Animal World

"Yes, I believe that the art of winning is through intimidation."

– Mark Spitz, Nine-Time Olympic Champion

You may have just read that title and thought "Wait, isn't that just a tired old cliché?" The fact is that most clichés contain a very real grain of truth. In life, generally, and in business, particularly, nice guys are lucky if they make it to the finish line at all and most can only dream of winning.

This has a lot to do with the makeup of the nature of all living things. In the ancient world, leaders and warriors often closely followed and mimicked the aggressive behaviors of certain "noble" animals, such as lions, tigers, bears and wolves.

Let me give you a potent example:

In studies of animal behavior in wolf packs, it's been established that perceived strength is not only necessary for success, it is also an absolute requirement for survival itself. While leading wolves hunt along with the rest of the pack, they are always allowed to eat their pick of the best part of the prey before the other wolves have even had a taste. This is because a leading wolf has managed to display its assertiveness by refusing to back down. Wolves regularly present challenges to one another in the form of an attack. If the wolf that has been challenged refuses to submit, a full-blown battle between the two animals will take place and the winner gains pack respect. A leading wolf is simply a wolf that has been challenged numerous times, has refused to back down each time, and has fought until the other wolf gave up.

All other wolves respect this leading wolf and as a result, its power over the pack is cemented. Now, by contrast, the weakest member of the pack is called the lowest subordinate. The lowest subordinate is exactly the opposite of the leading wolf. This type of wolf has lost all respect from its fellow pack members because when challenged, it was willing to submit. One single instance of submission is enough to earn a wolf the disdain of its fellow wolves for life. Once a wolf becomes a lowest subordinate, it can't rise from that level and its only option is to display "kind" or "likeable" characteristics to group members, in order to survive.

Lowest subordinate wolves often eat less than other wolves. They don't fight for space, resources or females and for a while, this kind of behavior allows them to pass unnoticed by the others. But at some point, pack members will remember their existence and will end up attacking them together. When a wolf pack attacks the lowest subordinate wolf together, they are using that weak wolf as a way to bond with one another and strengthen their group. This is similar to the way that a group of high school bullies will bond over an attack on another student they view as weak.

Unfortunately for the subordinate wolf, this type of attack can be brutal and often fatal. What's worse is that because the subordinate wolf has gotten so used to being "nice" for so long, it finds it impossible to defend itself when challenged by the group. In fact, you'll often see that these subordinate wolves lower themselves to the ground when attacked. This submissive pose is meant to elicit mercy from the others. However, with animals, just like with humans, overt submissiveness can often lead to even more ferocious attacks. Subordinate wolves who submit completely are often quickly killed.

In some cases, the subordinate will be backed into a corner and its natural animal survival instinct will awaken, causing it to snap and growl at its attackers. Surprisingly, when a subordinate does this, the other wolves immediately begin to back off. Why? Because they have just realized that this wolf may also fight back, if pushed too far. This small act of defiance earns the lowest subordinate wolf a little respect from the pack and that may just be enough to actually save its life.

Now, let's look at it from the human perspective.

Are you a human doormat? If you've always made it your policy to be nice- to customers who don't pay up, to colleagues who disrespect you or employees who fail to deliver, you are deeply harming yourself and the very foundations of your future wealth. Many business leaders will tell you: Nice is often just another name for someone who is too lazy to confront and deal with difficult situations. That's not how business is done and it's certainly not how money is made.

If you're a business owner, start today. With customers, set the tone by projecting a strong confident persona that people will be afraid to cross. Set your rules and don't budge, for any reason. Attempts to manipulate or disrespect you occur when others don't sense that you can and will react. If you have an ongoing relationship with a difficult or disrespectful client, it's difficult to change the entire tone once it's been set. I often advise clients to cut ties with those who have been disrespectful even once. That's because old behavior patterns in relationships never truly change. If you've made yourself a subordinate wolf in the eyes of a client, by allowing late or incomplete payment or bowing to unreasonable demands, it's likely that you will never be able to rebrand yourself into an equal, let alone a superior.

However, if the relationship is too important to sever, let your client know that you have many options and won't brook disrespect. Don't be afraid to do it. You'll lose less initially than you would by continuing to allow payment manipulation and other forms of client disrespect. This will actually positively impact your business, as your team will work better when they know that they have a leader they can look up to and count on.

With employees, make it clear that your requirements must be met. Those who fulfill your expectations will be rewarded. Those who do not will be punished. It's that simple.

Once those who work for you understand that "nice" will no longer be the default setting, you'll be amazed at how quickly productivity increases. Believe me-firmness works better than a million pep-talks, employee retreats and incentives.

Everyone knows of a co-worker who always goes out of their way to display a kind and friendly nature and a non-threatening stance to others. You know- "Fred" who allows others to leave the majority of the work to him, while they take all of the credit, or "Jane" who has become the target of workplace gossip and is too afraid to confront the matter head on.

These colleagues are often known for being "nice" but this doesn't save them from being misused, pushed around and generally disrespected by the very people who praise their kindness. In the cut-throat office environment, these co-workers have given away their power by refusing to react appropriately when dominated by their peers. Recently, a trend has emerged, with self-help books instructing people to remain as non-confrontational as possible in the workplace. These books claim that when you act with obvious goodwill, others will immediately respect you far more. The only problem with these books is that they assume that we humans have no connection to the kind of group mentality and power plays that animals engage in. They are essentially advising you to behave as a submissive subordinate, begging the pack to show you mercy.

Don't give away your power. I'm not advocating that you should ever start conflict in your workplace or business relationships. However, simply trying to avoid it by ignoring instances of abuses, harassment, lack of consideration or malicious gossip is the kiss of death to your career.

Conflict doesn't disappear when we ignore it. Instead, our refusal to address it in a timely manner actually signals fear and weakness to others-very often causing them to escalate their attacks and taking the conflict to a whole new and unwarranted level.

So what is the appropriate way to deal with attacks-whether they come from business partners, colleagues or even clients?

The first and most important step is to behave strategically. If you're going to show your power to others, it's best that you do so in a well-considered manner. Rage, shouting and threats may make an immediate impact but they are all signals that you have lost control of the situation-not a good message to send.

Instead, take a deep breath (that old cliché actually works!) and read the situation. 99% of the time, an attacker is hungry for an emotional reaction from you. Don't give it to them. Showing an opponent that you remain in control at all times is one of the most successful strategies for obtaining leader wolf status.

If, for example, an equal is lashing out at you because he/she wants to get a rise out of you, responding with undue emotion will leave that person eager for more and will end up making you appear "sensitive". While being "sensitive" to the feelings and actions of friends and loved ones is admirable, when it comes to dealing with others outside of this circle, it will place you in immediate and very real danger!

We've all seen a person react with so much rage that they actually end up getting choked up with angry tears. It's clear that the person is crying because of anger but that doesn't prevent them from looking like soft, pathetic, and ultimately, weak individuals.

On the other hand, if you've ever had the privilege of watching a real leader deal with an initial attack, then you've probably noticed that they remain completely collected, almost emotionless at first.

They often look their opponent dead in the eye and speak calmly, without any hint of fear, anger or anxiety.

So how would this apply to the theoretical situation above?

An ideal way to deal with a confrontation with someone who is in a peer-position to you is to immediately deal with the disrespect, without missing a beat.

Speak without raising your voice, but maintain a stern tone. Ask them whether they would like to state what their problem with you is. If not, then they should speak to you with respect, in order not to be disrespected themselves. This has done two very important things:

1. It has shown the offending person that you are neither afraid nor out of control. You've responded immediately to their behavior, but you've done so in a cool, calm collected way that also displays your complete control over the situation and your

emotions. Adults are no different from kids in this respect- emotional responses thrill and satisfy your attacker, causing them to want to continue to escalate the matter.

2. It has highlighted to the attacker and to all others who are listening that you can be counted on to ALWAYS stand up for yourself. Many people believe that they should walk away the first couple of times and only respond when it becomes unbearable. Time heals many things but it only aggravates workplace and business conflicts. To avoid the situation and wait for it to go away will only make the problematic person more likely to pull a similar or even worse stunt again. It will also alert others that you are probably unlikely to confront bad behavior, making you an easy target. In nature, easy targets don't survive and guess what? Office politics are no less hostile than the maneuverings found in wolf-infested woodlands.

When responding, remember to keep your tone commanding and emotionless, without raising your voice. This presents a "leading wolf" image and shows that the person is not capable of causing you to lose your cool. You've just shown your opponent that you are a superior- a person so far above them that their behavior can't get you worked up. Now, as we all know, when you behave as though you are superior, people around you have no choice but to believe that you have a reason for feeling that way. The effect of this response is to cause your opponent to freeze in their tracks and reconsider whether they really want to continue their actions.

The majority of attackers never expect to be confronted and when you upset their expectations by not only confronting them but doing so in a manner that highlights your superiority, they often choose to err on the side of caution and halt their attacks.

Will this approach always work and instantly put a stop to any future harassment?

Absolutely not-the simple truth is that the competitive nature of the world causes us to test, push and challenge one another, as we each desperately search for the resources we need. In a survival-based life, there will always be conflict and nowhere is this truer than when it comes to business, the workplace or anywhere where money is being made.

You will constantly be tested, but rest assured-every time you stand up for yourself, take the challenge and fight back you'll not only be establishing yourself as a leader to those around you, you'll also be preparing yourself to do battle and win.

It isn't fun, but nothing about adult life is a walk in the park. Your job is to get out there, meet the challenges head on and to protect and advance yourself every step of the way.

Every win will bring you a step closer to naturally behaving as, and becoming, a true warrior.

Also keep in mind that this doesn't necessarily apply to all conflicts. While standing up for yourself is easy enough to do when speaking to a colleague, it's admittedly a bit trickier when dealing with a disrespectful superior. I won't lie to you. There is no simple way to confront your boss or business superior. You're thrown into a situation where the roles are clearly defined by the fact that you receive pay or benefits from the other person, making it difficult to assert yourself as a superior, or even an equal, once conflict has started.

You can't deal with bullying from a professional superior in the same way outlined above. The plain, cold, hard fact is that if you are on the wrong end of disrespect from a boss or another person in a powerful position in relation to yours, the situation has already gone too far to fix. I don't say this to discourage you. Instead, I want to you to understand that when it comes to attacks from higher-ups, the key is not reaction but rather, prevention. The only strategy is to avoid being perceived as a victim from the very beginning.

I've outlined how to carry yourself and project an image of power and confidence in previous chapters and these tips are excellent for helping you to prevent a victim image when entering a new environment. The best way to prevent an attack from an opponent in a higher position is to set the right tone in all your dealings with them from the beginning.

We've all seen this scenario: "John" and "Julie" are both working on a project for a client. The client is well-known for being incredibly difficult and even rude, but he brings a great deal of business to the company, so both know they must make a good impression.

They each go about doing this in a different way. John assumes a deferential role. He opens doors for the client, fetches coffee for him without being asked, addresses him as "sir" at all times, eagerly laughs at all of his jokes and agrees enthusiastically with all of his opinions.

Julie takes a different approach. While she is unfailingly polite to the client, she also makes a point of focusing more on presenting excellent work than trying to "befriend" him. She may offer the client coffee, but she makes sure that her secretary brings it to him. She shows a professional level of respect for him but doesn't pander, call him "sir" or agree with his every word.

In fact, several times, she makes a point of calmly and confidently disagreeing with his opinions on the project and demonstrating her superior knowledge and experience. While John is clearly nervous and unsure of himself before the client, Julie maintains a cool, collected and matter-of-fact exterior.

While John tries desperately to "make the client like him", Julie works towards highlighting her expertise. As a result, the client treats each very differently. Because he perceives John's nervousness and eagerness to please as a lack of confidence, he has little confidence in him. He views John's laughter and agreement with his every word as "phony" and as a result, he does not trust him. And most importantly, he sees John's overly deferential manner as servile and because he takes it to mean that John views himself as inferior, he treats John accordingly.

With Julie on the other hand, the client assumes a totally separate role.

Because she is calm, confident and does not seek his "approval" on a personal level, he can't help but find himself approving of her. He views her assurance as a type of guarantee that she is competent, valuable and just as important as he is. He treats her accordingly.

Every signal, from needless laughter and pandering smiles, to fetching the coffee, is processed and used by the client to make a damning decision about John. Every message, from composure, business-like behavior and a refusal to be submissive, is processed and used by the client to make a positive decision about Julie.

In this scenario, John has made himself a subordinate wolf, while Julie has proved herself to be a leader wolf. What will your choice be?

People take us at our own estimation. In this way, we're similar to a shop, and the way we treat ourselves acts as a "price tag". People do not argue with our estimation of ourselves because they can read the "price tag". They know instantly what we are worth to them from sensing what we are worth to ourselves.

Chapter 9: How to Negotiate Like a Boss: Lessons Busines Warriors can Use to Win Every Battle

"In business, you don't get what you deserve, you get what you negotiate."
-Chester L Karrass, expert negotiator

In today's "softly, softly" world, there's a pervasive belief that the art of negotiation lies in the ability to give and take. Compromise has become the name of the game and we are told repeatedly that an all or nothing attitude will never get us what we want. But is it true?

Consider some of the greatest leaders of all time and you will see that they were not compromisers. They had a goal in mind and they used their powerful negotitation skills to ensure that they achieved that goal, and nothing less. Genghis Khan, the great Mongol ruler, dsiplayed these unbreakable negotiation tactics when taking a foregin territory. An envoy would be sent to the city under siege, telling the inhabitants that Genghis Khan would generoulsy offer them three choices:

1. They could surrender immediately to his superior force and this would earn them the right to continue to live. The city that surrendered immediately would be incorporated into the Great Mongol Empire.

2. If they waited even one day to obey Genghis Khan's command that they should surrender, he would take drastic steps. All males would be destroyed while the young and females would be allowed to live.

3. If they failed to surrender within the 2 day limit that the Khan set for them, they would all be destroyed, along with their entire city. Some cities thought that it would be alright for them to wait the 2 days and then come out to the Mongol forces with gifts and signs of surrender. They quickly found out that Genghis Khan was brutally and absolutely true to his word. No matter what they tried to do to appease him, the inhabitants of a city that failed to surrender within 2 days were all immediately and mercilessly wiped out. This was Genghis Khan's way of assuring everyone that met or heard of him that he was a man of his word and would never deviate from his decisions. And guess what? That made what could have been long, drawn out and difficult negotiations into a very simple process The people of any territory he came up against already knew that he would never budge an inch from his position so they often did whatever he commanded, without waiting an hour, let alone 2 days.

Although Genghis Khan's tactics were cruel and merciless, we can learn a great deal from them when it comes to the negotiation table. Regardless of what we've been told, business is not a game of accommodation or compromise-it's a very serious zero-sum battle and there is NO room for weakness, indecisiveness or lack of confidence.

So what makes a good negotiator? A bold, firm and cunning negotiator who understands the motivations and most importantly, the fears of those on the other side of the table is the only kind of negotiator who will walk away with victory firmly in hand.

With that in mind, I've gathered together the rules of negotiation like a true boss, so that you too, can walk away from talks having achieved the results you need.

Let's take a look:

Killer Negotiating Lesson #1: Intimidation is King:

I know that intimidation is stressed throughout this book but that is because it's truly one of the most powerful and pain-free methods of influencing others and achieving what you want.

Ever heard of the saying "speak softly and carry a big stick"? Well, I agree with it on all points, except, I would say "speak firmly and make sure your opponent thinks you've got the biggest stick".

That's because it's not really about how powerful you are in real terms. In fact, in business, you are only as powerful as those you're battling against think you are.

Whether you take your cues from Genghis Khan, charging down the plains with a force of thousands but creating enough dust to make it look to your opponents like you have a force of hundreds of thousands, or from Attila the Hun who greeted every envoy sent to him with a scowling, frightening expression that spoke of strength and power, although he was a short and physically unimposing man-the technique is the same: Make your opponent believe that you and your business are more than you really are, have more than you really have and can do far more than they can even imagine.

Killer Negotiating Lesson # 2: Lead Negotiations By Making Your Argument First: If you are negotiating for financial terms, the simplest and most effective way to ensure that you win is to go first. This is because the person who speaks first can mention their "anchor number". The anchor number is the number that you ideally want. When you state this number as your offer before the other side has had a chance to speak, you are, in essence, setting the tone for the negotiations

From that moment on, whatever number your opponent has in mind will immediately become viewed as relative to your number.

If your anchor number is high enough and you've created the intimidating and respect-gaining impression of wealth, power and self-respect, your opponent will be too afraid to mention a number that is drastically lower than the number you first mentioned.

Killer Negotiating Lesson #3: 2. Aim Higher Than You Need To:

Going for the absolute limit in negotiations may seem unreasonable and impractical but that's exactly why it works.

Stating a high number or a list of benefits as part of your demands immediately sets the tone, telling the other person that you are confident and powerful. In addition, it's a fact that starting negotiations on the high end frequently leads to a payoff higher than you expected. Don't be put off by the fact that the number you're about to state is considerably higher than what the other person is expecting. Your negotiation opponent doesn't know what you're really willing to accept or not.

Instead, focus on convincing yourself that this is a perfectly reasonable number and anything lower is unthinkable. This way, the minute you speak, your conviction will come through, making your opponent immediately truly believe that this is your final number. Your firmness will most likely shift the other's opinion towards yours, rather than allowing room for massive compromises that will harm your outcomes.

Killer Negotiating Lesson #4: Make Your Opponent Feel the Burden of a Time Crunch: Think about your average TV commercial: How often do the phrases "for a limited time only" or "while supplies last" make an appearance?

It's no secret that people desire things most when they believe that they won't be able to access them after time has passed. We all have FOMO (Fear of Missing Out) and nothing triggers us as much as the idea that a chance may pass us by.

The key to maneuvering through tricky negotiations is to make sure your opponent feels the full weight of a time-sensitive offer. Let your opponent know that the deal you're offering is only on the table for a limited period and that after that, you will be turning to other options or negotiations with other partners.

If you're selling a product or concept, let the opponent on the other end of the table know that there are plenty of potential buyers awaiting a shot at the same deal you're offering. Whether this is true or not doesn't matter. All that counts is that the statement is made as believably and confidently as possible, making it difficult to ignore.

Let's take a look at this example scenario:

Let's say you're selling shares in your new company and are meeting with an investor. You come in, perhaps wearing casual clothing that reflects your young startup roots, with a self-deprecating smile, fully aware of your own inexperience and of the investor's importance, wealth and power. You haven't convinced yourself of your own value, so you clearly display your insecurity, without meaning to.

Before you can even speak, the investor swoops in with a low-ball offer on the premise that you're a newbie with little experience and few options.

You can respond with anger, disbelief, or even a bold, flat out "No" but it's too late. You weren't able to initially establish your price and the fact that your company has plenty of would-be investors. You've been painted into a corner and it will be nearly impossible to claw your way out.

Now, let's look at the opposite scenario, this time with you using the killer negotiation skills you've learned:

Despite the fact that you're less experienced in negotiations, you've already prepared yourself not to present this in your meeting. You've shown both your self-respect and your confidence by dressing sharply and coaching yourself to believe that your company and your experience more than matches up to anything that the investor's got.

You come in with a strong, self-assured air that instantly makes you an equal and not a subordinate. You don't wait for the investor to low-ball you with an unsuitable offer. Instead, you calmly state your minimum price (though this price is much higher than what you may accept) and show clearly that you'll stick to your guns. You also let the investor know that your offer is time-sensitive.

Now, the investor has perceived your confidence, strength and your knowledge of your own value. He views you as an equal. This doesn't prevent him from trying to offer you a lower offer (though not as low as in the first scenario). When this happens however, you are prepared. You refuse, inform the investor that you have other offers and will now turn to those and make it clear that you're ready to leave if your offer is not matched.

Now the investor will begin to negotiate. This part is up to you and your true final number. Once the investor comes close enough to your final number to be acceptable, you can then seal the deal with a magnanimous handshake and leave the meeting with the knowledge that you've bluffed and dominated your way straight to the top.

From Genghis Khan to the business leaders of today, the best negotiators use human nature against itself.

Human nature forces us to respect those who appear to respect themselves. It also doesn't allow us to be comfortable with the idea that someone else may get a benefit or opportunity that we missed out on or mistakenly ignored. Use these very same facts to make your killer negotiations short, smooth and successful.

Chapter 10: Learning The Way of The Warrior From Alexander the Great and Genghis Khan: Make Discipline Your Discipline

"For a man to conquer himself is the first and noblest of all victories."
-Plato

Before Genghis Khan ruled them, the Mongols were already great horsemen and marauders. They were fierce, passionate and untamed and they descended upon their opponents with all the force of fury.

But they were also disorganized, divided and unable to utilize strategy for a greater cause than just gaining a little plunder.

They were so occupied with little skirmishes and feuds that they didn't have what it took to win great battles.

What Genghis Khan taught them was the way of the warrior- the way of discipline.

He took a disorganized bunch of feuding, scattered tribes and instilling in them his iron will, he turned them into a strong, unified force with the discipline to achieve his vision of conquering the world.

Old alliances and feuds were abolished and new rules held sway. Every male had to learn to ride and hunt from the age of 3 and all served in Genghis Khan's forces.

Luxury and extravagance was frowned upon and Genghis Khan ruled that gluttony and lack of restraint were crimes worthy of capital punishment. Every Mongolian man, woman and child thought, lived and breathed the way of the warrior.

Once, Genghis Khan and his men fought against an enormous force that clearly surpassed them in size and arms. Because Genghis Khan understood that his men would be absolutely decimated by this opposing force, he had his generals order his men to retreat. Usually, when a retreat occurred in the ancient world, the opposing forces would follow and destroy the retreating forces. However, in this case the forces opposing the Mongols didn't follow and attack them. Why?

Because Genghis Khan had formed such a tightly drilled, unified and disciplined force, that even when they were retreating they moved in complete unison. They did not run or scatter. Instead, they followed their orders perfectly and marched away with dignity and strength. Watching them leave, the leader of the other side was said to have told his forces not to follow the Mongols. He said if they were able to have such discipline when retreating, he did not want to have to face them in battle.

This is just one of the many ways in which discipline played a role in the successes of ancient warriors and it can have the very same effect on your life and financial future today.

Discipline is the single most important factor in success in all spheres of competition-whether in battle, sports or business. And if you don't have it, you will never achieve your true potential.

When author Thomas J. Stanley spoke with some of the men and women who are top 1% wealth holders in America, almost unanimously, they told him that the most important factor in their ability to create and maintain monumental wealth was their ability to be disciplined.

Why is Discipline So Critical For the Business Warrior?

Whether you're Genghis Khan, carefully planning, building a force and conquering foreign lands, Alexander the Great, pouring your effort into a harsh and difficult warrior's education or a business person in today's tough economy, struggling to build your dream into a future of financial success and freedom- discipline is the key to your victory.

As we know, everything of real value must be hard-won. So often, I speak with people who want to discuss their ambitions and business goals with me. They spend a great deal of time outlining the successful outcome of their plans but very little time explaining the difficult steps they will take to reach that outcome. One of the saddest outcomes of an ever-more physically comfortable world is that we live in an age where the idea of discipline or the practice of doing the tough things that will lead us to our goals every day, has completely disappeared.

We crave results but too often, we have no idea what it takes to really get them. It's because of this that I wanted to devote an entire section to the concept of discipline. I truly believe that no other factor can have half the impact on your business success and your continued ability to create and keep wealth that discipline will and I want to share with you valuable examples of the ways in which ancient warriors used extreme discipline to get extreme results.

Alexander the Great of Macedon:

Alexander the Great, one of the greatest empire builders and warriors our world has ever known, was born into a position of great privilege, as the son of King Philip of Macedon. By any standards, he should have grown up to be a spoiled, weak-willed and incapable young man. Instead, he became one of the toughest, most competent leaders in history, leading powerful forces and conquering all of Persia, large parts of the Middle East, Mesopotamia, Bactria, and the Punjab before the age of 32!

Because Alexander the Great grew up in a warrior-society that rejected excessive comfort and luxury, he was able to cultivate a strong sense of discipline that aided him in achieving his almost impossible goals.

In fact, In Alexander's time, Macedonian forces would sometimes drill and march for over 30 miles in a single day! And so strict and harsh was the discipline of the society that a warrior bathing in warm water would immediately be stripped of his title and expelled. Even Macedonian women who had just given birth were not permitted to bathe in warm water, as it was considered undisciplined and self-indulgent to do so!

In addition, Alexander was raised to endure the harsh schooling of Leonidas, his mother's brother. Leonidas was incredibly stern with the young man, mercilessly instilling in him the tough mind-set that turned him into a master warrior. It was the combination of all of these brutal circumstances that contributed to his incredible victories over much of the ancient world.

So how can you harness the power that made Alexander the Great the sole ruler of immense territories for your own business and life?

Begin with Responsibility:

Everyone understands the importance of responsibility, but no one wants to have to take it upon themselves. And that's because it's heavy. Responsibility is a huge burden. Learning to make promises and keep them, fulfilling what's required of you, when it's required of you and without complaint can be the toughest step in the process of becoming a successful business warrior. That's why it's the step that 99.9% of those who want to be rich and accomplished fail at.

Once you get past responsibility, you can be sure that your goal is closer than ever.

Start your journey by keeping the promise you make to yourself, whether small or big. If you say you're going to go for a run, go for a run, if you're going to quit smoking, throw the pack away. If you begin by keeping your personal promises to yourself, you'll start to view yourself as a trustworthy and committed person, and that makes all the difference. You'll find yourself increasingly reluctant to break promises or sabotage your success with excuses, once you begin to believe in the idea of a strong, responsible you.

Next, work towards being a person people know they can count on. When you say you'll do something, don't procrastinate, don't make excuses and don't postpone, just do it. Your word is as valuable as the strength and depth of your sense of responsibility. Your business reputation, once broken, can never be repaired. Make sure that when people hear or see you, they hear and see integrity. Let responsibility be your brand. It will serve you well.

Now is this easy? Not at all-it's actually a huge burden. But just remember this: burdens are what make your success.

Take the men who marched to victory under Alexander the Great as your personal example. They each had to carry enough supplies to last up to 30 days on the road, as they marched from region to region.

Were these loads heavy? Sure. But they ended up actually strengthening and training the men with every step they took, directly leading to their victories across the world. That's exactly what taking on the burden of responsibility will do for you.

As the well-known rags-to-riches American success story Jim Rohn said "There are two types of pain you will go through in life, the pain of discipline and the pain of regret. Discipline weighs ounces, while regret weighs tons."

It's up to you: Carry ounces today or pay in tons of regret tomorrow.

Start today. You'll be bringing your future victory much closer with every step you take.

Delay Your Desire:

We live in a fast world. Instant thrills and instant gratification may be fun, but they won't make you rich or powerful.

The ancient world was far less addicted to quick pay offs. Instead, the people of the past understood what too many of us have forgotten today. Nothing worth having comes quickly.

Discipline is really the act of doing what must be done every day, whether you want to or not. The discipline of delaying your desire takes it a step further. It requires you NOT to do what you want to do, if it will distance you from your goal. Every day, you've got to get up and decide to avoid the momentary pleasures that may keep you from achieving financial freedom. So, if you enjoy gambling or you love to splurge on shopping, delay your desire in order to put that money towards your business. In the long-term, you'll see the money that might have been wasted on cheap thrills grow into something that supports you and allows you to be independent and free.

Getting too wrapped up in feeding our temporary appetites can delay or destroy our financial futures. As Genghis Khan once explained, these desires can easily distract us and diminish our focus: "I hate luxury. I exercise moderation…It will be easy to forget your vision and purpose one you have fine clothes, fast horses and beautiful women. [In which case], you will be no better than a slave, and you will surely lose everything."

Don't Wait For the Perfect Time:

What's the perfect moment to start out on the road to business success? The answer will always be today, right now, right here. We're very often caught up in the idea of something "feeling right". I've got news for you. Change is always unpleasant and change involving increasing your discipline can be downright painful. That's ok. Discipline is supposed to hurt. That's how you know it's really working.

If Alexander the Great had waited for the perfect moment, he would have turned back many times from some of his most daring conquests. Instead, he used the discipline and determination of a soldier to keep marching towards the victory, every day, all of the time.

Your habits are governed by an area within your brain called your basal ganglia, while your conscious decisions are made within your brain's prefrontal cortex. These two areas are completely different, so when you go from automatically doing what you're used to doing to consciously making a choice to do something different such as make disciplined decisions, you'll feel slightly off. When you repeatedly give into your habits, you're programming your brain to work in this way all the time so the switch to conscious actions won't be easy for your brain to handle. The cure is persistence, as we all know that doing something new for 21 days makes it your new habit. Don't give up or decide to wait for a better time. Replace old undisciplined habits with new ways of doing things that make your road to success shorter.

Be Consistent:

While the most important part of your business warrior strategy is discipline, the most essential component of your discipline must be consistency. The best warriors are not defined by one battle or heroic moment. Instead, their legacies are built from using their discipline to do difficult, challenging things every day, keeping their word and saying "no" to the temptations that could sidetrack their success.

By the time he had taken his last breath, Alexander the Great's forces had each travelled almost 21,000 miles, crossing raging rivers, endless scorching desserts, scaling dizzying mountains and braving both freezing winters and burning summers. They are the perfect epitome of consistency. While they fought legendary battles, it was the daily act of putting one foot in front of the other and moving forward that made their amazing victories possible. So keep going. Be committed and consistent with all of the habits and steps outlined in this book.

Alexander's forces guaranteed their victory by continually proving themselves through tough daily action. The same will be true for your business success. So start marching with discipline today. You'll be bringing your future victory much closer with every step you take.

Conclusion:

Thank you for joining me on this journey into the ancient past to uncover and examine the secrets of legendary warriors. As you've seen, every single one of these strategies is highly adaptable to modern life and able to help you on your path to becoming a full-fledged business warrior. From protecting yourself to projecting an image of strength, from negotiating to win to reinforcing your sense of self-discipline the psychological strategies of ancient warriors like Genghis Khan, Attila the Hun and Alexander the Great are ideal for helping you to win in this difficult business environment.

Whether you're a first-time entrepreneur, an established business owner or simply want to work your way up the ranks at your current job, use the strategies of intimidation, confidence, image branding, power plays and strict discipline to win the financial freedom you seek.

Take these secrets, skills and strategies out of the past and apply them to your daily life today, to gain power over yourself, influence others and create the business success of your dreams.

In closing, I leave you with a powerful quote from Alexander the Great:

"Through every generation of the human race there has been a constant war, a war with fear. Those who have the courage to conquer it are made free and those who are conquered by it are made to suffer until they have the courage to defeat it, or death takes them. "

-Alexander the Great

Remember that although achieving your goals may be tiring and difficult, you have to go forward without fear. Fear paralyzes, fear postpones and fear destroys.

No one is going to give you your financial freedom. You have to take it yourself, with both hands and without hesitation. Every single day, train internally for your external challenges and remember that once you've conquered yourself, your goals grow closer than ever.

While the road to your final financial victory is long, you've taken the first steps with this book. I wish you good luck, strength, discipline, and success in all of your business battles!

CPSIA information can be obtained
at www.ICGtesting.com
Printed in the USA
LVOW13s1718210817
545807LV00035B/1235/P